Index Of Leading Catholic Indicators

The Church Since Vatican II

Kenneth C. Jones

Index of Leading Catholic Indicators

Copyright 2003

ISBN 1-929291-58-2

Roman Catholic Books
Post Office Box 2286, Fort Collins, CO 80522
BooksforCatholics.com

Acknowledgments

I wish to thank Roger A. McCaffrey for his role in the development of this project and Dr. James R. Lothian, Distinguished Professor of Finance at Fordham University and editor of the Journal of International Money and Finance, for contributing the statistical projections of priests, sisters, brothers and priestless parishes.

The book is dedicated to my wife, Claudia, whose love and support made it all possible.

Do you ever pick grapes from thornbushes, or figs from prickly plants? Any sound tree bears good fruit, while a decayed tree bears bad fruit. A sound tree cannot bear bad fruit any more than a decayed tree can bear good fruit. Every tree that does not bear good fruit is cut down and thrown into the fire. You can tell a tree by its fruit.
Matt. 7: 16-21

Deus, tu conversus vivificabis nos.
Et plebs tua laetabitur in te.
O God, Thou wilt turn again and give us life.
And thy people shall rejoice in Thee.
Psalm 84
The Roman Missal of 1962

Contents

Introduction	7
Chapter 1 — Priests and Religious	13
Chapter 2 — Catholic Education	39
Chapter 3 — Catholic Practice and Belief	63
Chapter 4 — Religious Orders	83
Chapter 5 — Canada and Europe	103

6   Index of Leading Catholic Indicators

Introduction

When Pope John XXIII opened the Second Vatican Council in 1962, the Catholic Church in America was in the midst of an unprecedented period of growth.

Bishops were ordaining record numbers of priests and building scores of seminaries to handle the surge in vocations. Young women by the thousands gave up lives of comfort for the austerity of the convent. These nuns taught millions of students in the huge system of parochial and private schools.

The ranks of Catholics swelled as parents brought in their babies for baptism and adult converts flocked to the Church. Lines outside the confessionals were long, and by some estimates three quarters of the faithful went to Mass every Sunday.

Given this favorable state of affairs, some Catholics wondered at the time whether an ecumenical council was opportune – don't rock the boat, they said.

The Holy Father chided these people in his opening speech to the Council: "We feel we must disagree with those prophets of gloom, who are always forecasting disaster, as though the end of the world were at hand."

Forty years later the end has not arrived. But we are now facing the disaster.

Even some in the Vatican have recognized it. Cardinal Joseph Ratzinger, prefect of the Congregation for the Doctrine of the Faith, said: "Certainly the results (of Vatican II) seem cruelly opposed to the expectations of everyone, beginning with those of Pope John XXIII and then of Pope Paul VI: expected was a new Catholic unity and instead we have been exposed to dissension which, to use the words of Pope Paul VI, seems to have gone from self-criticism to self-destruction. Expected was a new enthusiasm, and many wound up discouraged and bored.

"Expected was a great step forward, instead we find ourselves faced with a progressive process of decadence which has developed for the most part under the sign of a calling back to the Council, and has therefore contributed to discrediting it for many. The net result therefore seems negative. I am repeating here what I said ten years after the conclusion of the work: it is incontrovertible that this period has definitely been unfavorable for the Catholic Church."

Since Cardinal Ratzinger made these remarks in 1984, the crisis in the Church has accelerated. In every area that is statistically verifiable – for example, the number of priests, seminarians, priestless parishes, nuns, Mass attendance, converts and annulments – the "process of decadence" is apparent.

I have gathered these statistics in The Index of Leading Catholic Indicators because the magnitude of the emergency is unknown to many. Beyond a vague understanding of a "vocations crisis," both the faithful and the general public have no idea how bad things have been since the close of the Second Vatican Council in 1965.

Here are some of the stark facts.

• **Priests.** After skyrocketing from about 27,000 in 1930 to 58,000 in 1965, the number of priests in the United States dropped to 45,000 in 2002. By 2020, there will be about 31,000 priests – and only 15,000 will be under the age of 70. Right now there are more priests age 80 to 84 than there are age 30 to 34.

• **Ordinations.** In 1965 there were 1,575 ordinations to the priesthood, in 2002 there were 450, a decline of 350 percent. Taking into account ordinations, deaths and departures, in 1965 there was a net gain of 725 priests. In 1998, there was a net loss of 810.

• **Priestless parishes.** About 1 percent of parishes, 549, were without a resident priest in 1965. In 2002 there were 2,928 priestless parishes, about 15 percent of U.S. parishes. By 2020, a quarter of all parishes, 4,656, will have no priest.

• **Seminarians.** Between 1965 and 2002, the number of seminarians dropped from 49,000 to 4,700 – a 90 percent decrease. Without any students, seminaries across the country have been sold or shuttered. There were 596 seminaries in 1965, and only 200 in 2002.

• **Sisters.** 180,000 sisters were the backbone of the Catholic education and health systems in 1965. In 2002, there were 75,000 sisters, with an average age of 68. By 2020, the number of sisters will drop to 40,000 – and of these, only 21,000 will be age 70 or under. In 1965, 104,000 sisters were teaching, while in 2002 there were only 8,200 teachers.

• **Brothers.** The number of professed brothers decreased from about 12,000 in 1965 to 5,700 in 2002, with a further drop to 3,100 in 2020.

• **Religious Orders.** The religious orders will soon be virtually non-existent in the United States. For example, in 1965 there were 5,277 Jesuit priests and 3,559 seminarians; in 2000 there were 3,172 priests and 389 seminarians. There were 2,534 OFM Franciscan priests and 2,251 seminarians in 1965; in 2000 there were 1,492 priests and 60 seminarians. There were 2,434 Christian Brothers in 1965 and 912 seminarians; in 2000 there were 959 Brothers and 7 seminarians. There were 1,148 Redemptorist priests in 1965 and 1,128 seminarians; in 2000 there were 349 priests and 24 seminarians. Every major religious order in the United States mirrors these statistics.

• **High Schools.** Between 1965 and 2002 the number of diocesan high schools fell from 1,566 to 786. At the same time the number of students dropped from almost 700,000 to 386,000.

• **Parochial Grade Schools.** There were 10,503 parochial grade schools in 1965 and 6,623 in 2002. The number of students went from 4.5 million to 1.9 million.

• **Sacramental Life.** In 1965 there were 1.3 million infant baptisms, in 2002 there were 1 million. (In the same period the number of Catholics in the United States rose from 45 million to 65 million.) In 1965 there were 126,000 adult baptisms – converts – in 2002 there were 80,000. In 1965 there were 352,000 Catholic marriages, in 2002 there were 256,000. In 1968 there were 338 annulments, in 2002 there were 50,000.

• **Mass attendance.** A 1958 Gallup poll reported that 74 percent of Catholics went to Sunday Mass in 1958. A 1994 University of Notre Dame study found that the attendance rate was 26.6 percent. A more recent study by Fordham University professor James Lothian concluded that 65 percent of Catholics went to Sunday Mass in 1965, while the rate dropped to 25 percent in 2000.

The decline in Mass attendance highlights another significant fact – fewer and fewer people who call themselves Catholic actually follow Church rules or accept Church doctrine. For example, a 1999 poll by the National

Catholic Reporter shows that 77 percent believe a person can be a good Catholic without going to Mass every Sunday, 65 percent believe good Catholics can divorce and remarry, and 53 percent believe Catholics can have abortions and remain in good standing. Only 10 percent of lay religion teachers accept Church teaching on artificial birth control, according to a 2000 University of Notre Dame poll. And a New York Times/CBS poll revealed that 70 percent of Catholics age 18-44 believe the Eucharist is merely a "symbolic reminder" of Jesus.

Given these alarming statistics and surveys, one wonders why the American bishops ignore the profound crisis that threatens the very existence of the Church in America. After all, there can be no Church without priests, no Church without a laity that has children and practices the Catholic faith.

Yet at their annual conferences, the bishops gather to issue weighty statements about nuclear weapons and the economy. Then they return home to "consolidate" parishes and close down schools.

As Cardinal Ratzinger said, the post-Vatican II period "has definitely been unfavorable for the Catholic Church." This Index of Leading Catholic Indicators is an attempt to chronicle the continuing crisis, in the hope that a compilation of the grim statistics – in a clear, objective, easy to understand manner – will spur action before it is too late.

Kenneth C. Jones
January 2003

❖ *Between 1965 and 2002, total U.S. Catholics increased by 43 percent.*

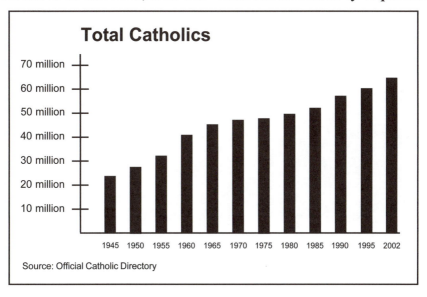

Total Catholics	
Year	Catholics
1920	17,735,553
1930	20,203,702
1940	21,403,136
1945	23,963,671
1950	27,766,141
1955	32,575,702
1960	40,871,302
1965	45,640,619
1970	47,872,089
1975	48,701,835
1980	49,660,577
1985	52,286,043
1990	57,019,948
1995	60,190,605
2002	65,270,444

Source: Official Catholic Directory

Chapter 1

Priests and Religious

❖ *Between 1965 and 2002, the number of total U.S. priests declined from 58,632 to 45,713, a decrease of 22 percent, and will drop to 30,992 in 2020.*

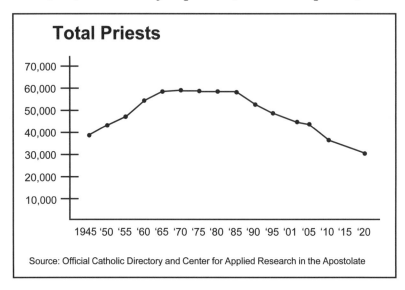

❖ *In 1965 there were 12.85 total priests for every 10,000 Catholics, in 2002 there were 7.00 — a decline of 46 percent.*

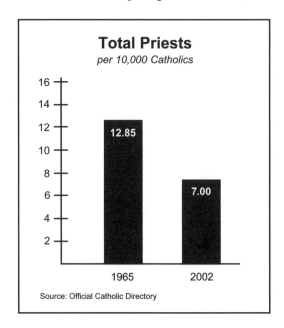

Total Priests

Year	Priests	Percentage Increase (Decrease)
1920	21,019	-
1930	26,925	28%
1940	33,912	26%
1945	38,451	13%
1950	42,970	12%
1955	46,970	09%
1960	53,796	15%
1965	58,632	09%
1970	59,192	01%
1975	58,909	(01%)
1980	58,621	(01%)
1985	57,317	(02%)
1990	53,111	(07%)
1995	49,947	(06%)
2002	45,713	(08%)
2005	44,874	(02%)
2010	37,624	(16%)
2020	30,992	(18%)

Source: Official Catholic Directory

❖ There were approximately 27,000 priests in active parish ministry in 2000. (*Executive Summary: The Study of the Impact of Fewer Priests on the Pastoral Ministry*, United States Conference of Catholic Bishops, June 2000)

❖ The average age of priests in the United States in 2000 was 57 years for diocesan priests, and 63 years for religious priests. There were 433 priests over the age of 90 and 298 priests under the age of 30. (*The Study of the Impact of Fewer Priests*)

❖ Sixteen percent of all the priests active in parish ministry come from other countries. (*The Study of the Impact of Fewer Priests*)

❖ "In the past year, some 325 of the nation's 46,000 priests have resigned or been removed from ministry because of sex-abuse allegations." (U.S. News and World Report, Nov. 25, 2002).

❖ *By 2020, there will be only 15,235 priests age 70 and under.*

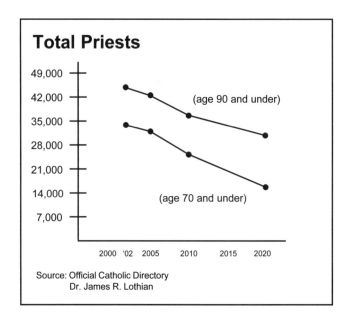

Total Priests

Year	Priests Age 90 and under	Priests Age 70 and under
2002	44,874	34,164
2005	42,487	31,665
2010	37,624	25,743
2020	30,992	15,235

Source: Official Catholic Directory
Dr. James R. Lothian

Priests and Religious

Total Priests — Net Change
Ordinations, Deaths and Departures

Year	Ordinations	Deaths	Departures	Net Change
1960	1,527	650	75	802
1965	1,575	725	125	725
1970	1,245	750	675	(180)
1975	1,136	850	425	(139)
1980	883	810	260	(187)
1985	748	905	230	(387)
1990	620	945	215	(540)
1995	520	965	265	(710)
1998	460	1,040	230	(810)

Source: Catholicism USA: A Portrait of the Catholic Church in the United States

❖ "In recent years the number of retired diocesan priests has gradually increased from 6,436 in 1990 to 7,785 by 1999, according to the [Official Catholic Directory]. Should this current pattern continue, the retired population of diocesan priests will increase to 8,107 by 2005. The increase in the number of retirees has occurred at a time when the total of diocesan priests declined from 32,992 in 1990 to 30,034 by 1999 and a forecast of 27,940 by 2005. The proportion of retired diocesan priests as a part of the total clergy population has increased from 19.5 percent in 1990 to 24 percent and will likely grow to a forecast of 29 percent by 2005." (*The Shrinking Supply of Priests*, Joseph Claude Harris, *America*, Nov. 4, 2000)

❖ "From 1995 through 1999, there were 1,247 diocesan ordinations according to the [Official Catholic Directory], but there were also 2,654 deaths or resignations from the priesthood. ... In short, the ordination classes would need to double in size to keep up with the decline caused by deaths and resignations." (*The Shrinking Supply of Priests*, Joseph Claude Harris, *America*, Nov. 4, 2000)

Priests and Parish Life

❖ *Between 1965 and 2002, priestless parishes increased from 549 to 2,928, a jump of more than 500 percent, and will grow to 4,656 in 2020.*

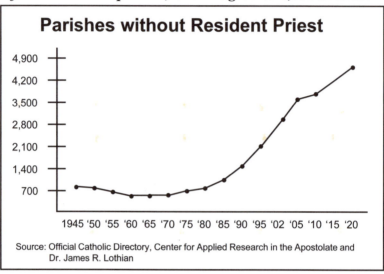

Parishes without Resident Priest

Source: Official Catholic Directory, Center for Applied Research in the Apostolate and Dr. James R. Lothian

Parishes without Resident Priest

Year	Parishes	Percentage Increase (Decrease)
1945	839	-
1950	791	(06%)
1955	673	(15%)
1960	546	(19%)
1965	549	01%
1970	571	04%
1975	702	23%
1980	791	13%
1985	1,051	33%
1990	1,507	43%
1995	2,161	43%
2002	2,928	35%
2005	3,586	22%
2010	3,831	07%
2020	4,656	22%

Source: Official Catholic Directory, Center for Applied Research in the Apostolate and Dr. James R. Lothian

Priests and Religious

❖ "For a parish to have a priest as its own pastor is of fundamental importance. The title of pastor is one specifically reserved to the priest. ... Other faithful may actively collaborate with him, even full time, but, as he has received the ministerial priesthood, they can never take his place as pastor. ... The ecclesial community absolutely needs the ministerial priesthood to have Christ Head and Pastor in it. ... [The non-ordained] must be faithful to their proper function as consultants and care must be taken that no office or person deprive the parish priest of his authority." (John Paul II, Vatican Information Service, Nov. 23, 2001)

❖ *Between 1965 and 2001, the percentage of priestless parishes increased by more than 500 percent. By 2020, one quarter of all parishes will be priestless.*

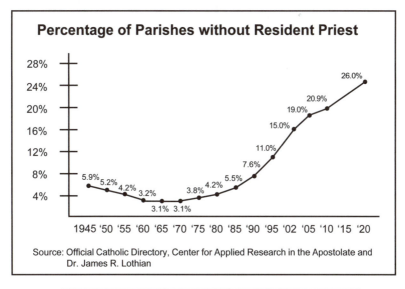

Percentage of Parishes without Resident Priest

1945: 5.9%, '50: 5.2%, '55: 4.2%, '60: 3.2%, '65: 3.1%, '70: 3.1%, '75: 3.8%, '80: 4.2%, '85: 5.5%, '90: 7.6%, '95: 11.0%, '02: 15.0%, '05: 19.0%, '10: 20.9%, '20: 26.0%

Source: Official Catholic Directory, Center for Applied Research in the Apostolate and Dr. James R. Lothian

Number of Parishes

Year	Parishes	Year	Parishes
1945:	14,302	1985:	19,244
1950:	15,292	1990:	19,860
1955:	16,035	1995:	19,723
1960:	16,896	2002:	19,093
1965:	17,637	2005:	18,823
1970:	18,224	2010:	18,373
1975:	18,515	2020:	17,923
1980:	18,794		

Source: Official Catholic Directory, Center for Applied Research in the Apostolate and Dr. James R. Lothian

❖ *Between 1965 and 2002, the number of U.S. diocesan priests decreased by 15 percent. There were more diocesan priests in 1960 than in 2002.*

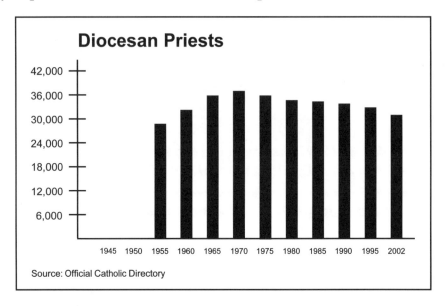

❖ *In 1965 there were 7.87 diocesan priests for every 10,000 Catholics, in 2002 there were 4.66 — a decline of 41 percent.*

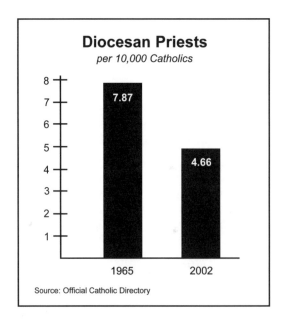

Diocesan Priests

Year	Priests	Percentage Increase (Decrease)
1920	15,389	-
1930	18,873	23%
1940	22,450	19%
1945	N/A	-
1950	N/A	-
1955	28,873	-
1960	32,569	13%
1965	35,925	10%
1970	37,272	04%
1975	36,005	(03%)
1980	35,418	(02%)
1985	35,052	(01%)
1990	34,553	(01%)
1995	32,834	(05%)
2002	30,429	(07%)

Source: Official Catholic Directory

❖ Reducing the number of Masses as a response to the decline in the number of priests was a strategy used "somewhat" or "very much" by 42 percent of the dioceses in 2000; 69 percent of the dioceses expected to do this within 10 years. (*The Study of the Impact of Fewer Priests*)

❖ "In recent years the number of retired diocesan priests has gradually increased from 6,436 in 1990 to 7,785 by 1999, according to the [Official Catholic Directory]. Should this current pattern continue, the retired population of diocesan priests will increase to 8,107 by 2005. (*The Shrinking Supply of Priests*, Joseph Claude Harris, *America*, Nov. 4, 2000)

❖ *Between 1965 and 2002, the number of U.S. religious priests decreased by 33 percent. There were more religious priests in 1955 than in 2002.*

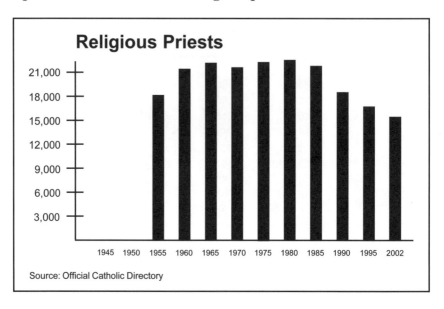

❖ *In 1965 there were 4.98 religious priests for every 10,000 Catholics, in 2002 there were 2.34 — a decline of 53 percent.*

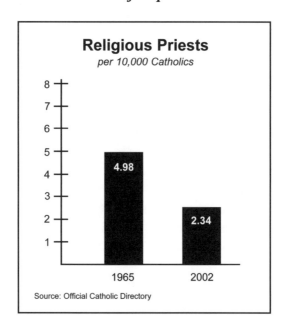

Religious Priests

Year	Priests	Percentage Increase (Decrease)
1920	5,630	-
1930	8,052	43%
1940	11,462	42%
1945	N/A	-
1950	N/A	-
1955	18,097	-
1960	21,227	17%
1965	22,707	07%
1970	21,920	(03%)
1975	22,904	04%
1980	23,203	01%
1985	22,265	(04%)
1990	18,559	(17%)
1995	16,717	(10%)
2002	15,244	(09%)

Source: Official Catholic Directory

❖ *In 1999 there were more total U.S. priests in the 65 to 69 age group than in any other five-year age group. There were more priests age 80 to 84 than age 30 to 34.*

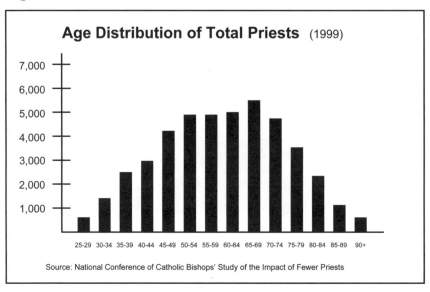

❖ *In 1999 there were more diocesan priests in the 65 to 69 age group than in any other five-year age group. There were more diocesan priests age 80 to 84 than age 30 to 34.*

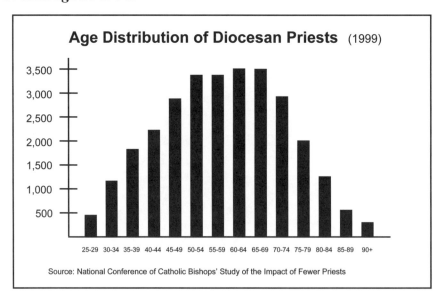

❖ *In 1999 there were more religious priests in the 65 to 69 age group than in any other five-year age group. There were more religious priests age 80 to 84 than age 30 to 34.*

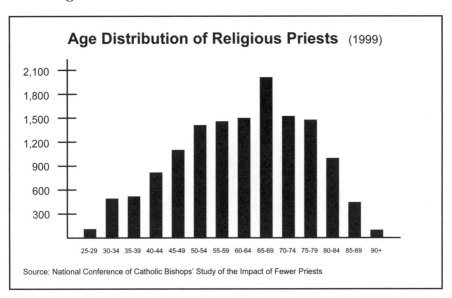

❖ "[O]nly 29 percent of priests were 55 or older in 1966. By 1985 ... the clergy population aged notably with 40 percent of priests age 55 or older. [In 1998] we estimate that 45 percent of priests are in this oldest age group and that in 2005, 46 percent of priests will belong to the group age 55 or older." (*Adddressing and Updating the Schoenherr-Young Projections of Clergy Decline in teh United States Roman Catholic Church*, Lawrence A. Young, *The Sociology Of Religion*, Spring 2000)

Seminarians

❖ *Between 1965 and 2002, the number of total U.S. seminarians decreased by 90 percent. There were over three times as many seminarians in 1930 as in 2002.*

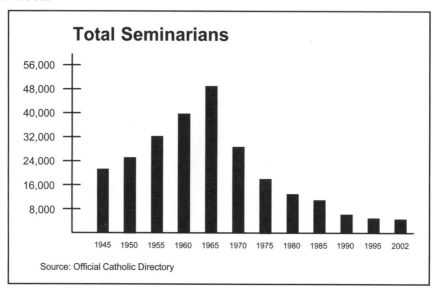

❖ *In 1965 there were 10.73 total seminarians for every 10,000 Catholics, in 2002 there was .72 — a decline of 93 percent.*

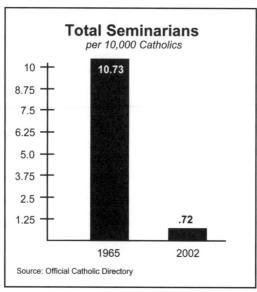

Total Seminarians

Year	Seminarians	Percentage Increase (Decrease)
1920	8,944	-
1930	16,300	82%
1940	17,087	05%
1945	21,523	26%
1950	25,622	19%
1955	32,394	26%
1960	39,896	23%
1965	48,992	23%
1970	28,819	(41%)
1975	17,802	(38%)
1980	13,226	(26%)
1985	11,028	(17%)
1990	6,233	(43%)
1995	5,083	(18%)
2002	4,719	(07%)

Source: Official Catholic Directory

❖ The average age of seminarians in 1965 was 25; in 1993 it was 32. (*Seminarians in the Nineties*, National Catholic Education Association, 1993)

❖ *Between 1965 and 2002, the number of diocesan seminarians decreased by 88 percent. There were over three times as many diocesan seminarians in 1945 as in 2002.*

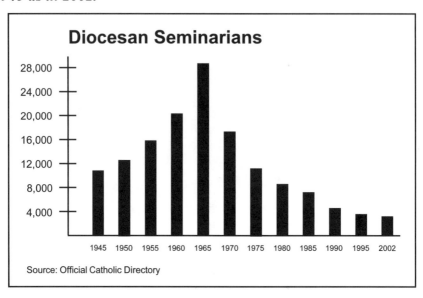

❖ *In 1965 there were 6.30 diocesan seminarians for every 10,000 Catholics, in 2002 there was .51 — a decline of 92 percent.*

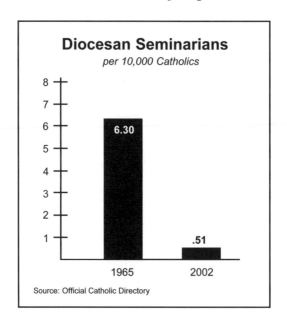

Diocesan Seminarians

Year	Seminarians	Percentage Increase (Decrease)
1945	11,043	-
1950	12,464	13%
1955	15,901	28%
1960	20,278	28%
1965	28,762	42%
1970	17,317	(40%)
1975	11,223	(35%)
1980	8,552	(24%)
1985	7,277	(15%)
1990	4,447	(39%)
1995	3,522	(21%)
2002	3,359	(05%)

Source: Official Catholic Directory

❖ *Between 1965 and 2002, the number of religious seminarians decreased by 95 percent. There were over seven times as many religious seminarians in 1945 as in 2002.*

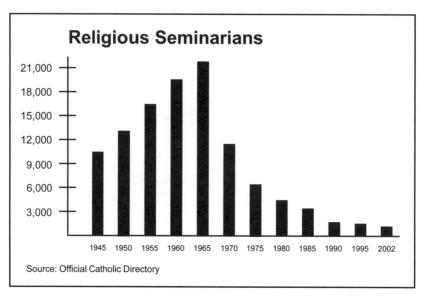

❖ *In 1965 there were 4.87 religious seminarians for every 10,000 Catholics, in 2002 there was .21 — a decline of 96 percent.*

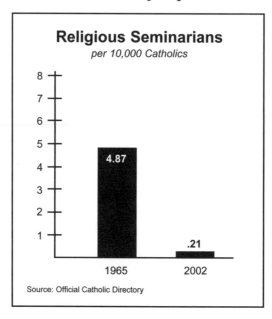

Religious Seminarians

Year	Seminarians	Percentage Increase (Decrease)
1945	10,480	-
1950	13,158	26%
1955	16,493	25%
1960	19,618	19%
1965	22,230	13%
1970	11,589	(48%)
1975	6,579	(43%)
1980	4,674	(29%)
1985	3,751	(20%)
1990	1,786	(52%)
1995	1,561	(13%)
2002	1,360	(13%)

Source: Official Catholic Directory

Seminaries

❖ *Between 1965 and 2002, the number of U.S. diocesan seminaries decreased by 33 percent. There were more seminaries in 1955 than in 2002.*

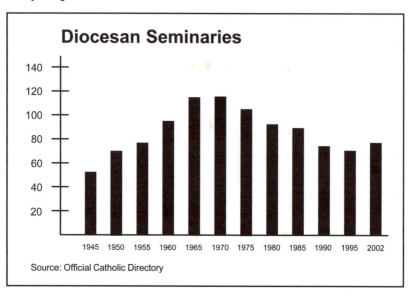

Diocesan Seminaries

Year	Seminaries	Percentage Increase (Decrease)
1945	53	-
1950	72	36%
1955	78	08%
1960	96	23%
1965	117	22%
1970	118	01%
1975	104	(12%)
1980	92	(12%)
1985	90	(02%)
1990	75	(17%)
1995	72	(04%)
2002	78	08%

Source: Official Catholic Directory

❖ *Between 1965 and 2002, the number of U.S religious seminaries decreased by 75 percent. There were more than twice as many seminaries in 1945 as in 2002.*

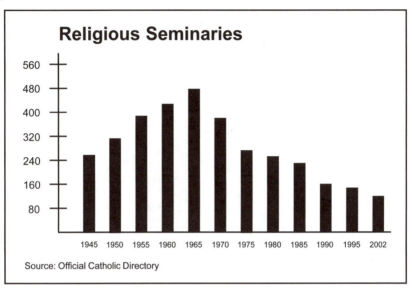

Religious Seminaries

Year	Seminaries	Percentage Increase (Decrease)
1945	258	-
1950	316	22%
1955	385	22%
1960	429	11%
1965	479	12%
1970	383	(20%)
1975	269	(30%)
1980	252	(06%)
1985	228	(10%)
1990	159	(30%)
1995	146	(08%)
2002	122	(16%)

Source: Official Catholic Directory

Brothers

❖ *Between 1965 and 2002, the number of brothers declined from 12,271 to 5,690, a decrease of 54 percent, and will drop to 3,098 in 2020.*

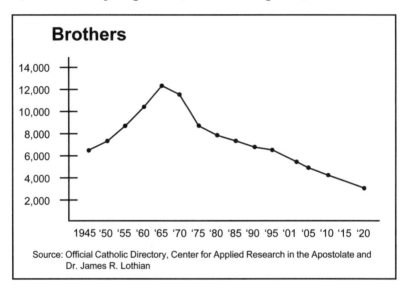

❖ *In 1965 there were 2.69 brothers for every 10,000 Catholics, in 2002 there was .87 — a decline of 68 percent.*

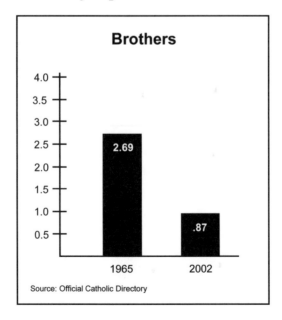

Brothers

Year	Brothers	Percentage Increase (Decrease)
1945	6,594	-
1950	7,377	12%
1955	8,752	19%
1960	10,473	20%
1965	12,271	17%
1970	11,623	(05%)
1975	8,625	(26%)
1980	7,941	(08%)
1985	7,544	(05%)
1990	6,743	(11%)
1995	6,578	(02%)
2002	5,690	(13%)
2005	5,031	(12%)
2010	4,288	(15%)
2020	3,098	(28%)

Source: Official Catholic Directory, Center for Applied Research in the Apostolate and Dr. James R. Lothian

Sisters

❖ *Between 1965 and 2002, the number of sisters declined from 179,954 to 75,500, a decrease of 58 percent, and will drop to 39,282 in 2020.*

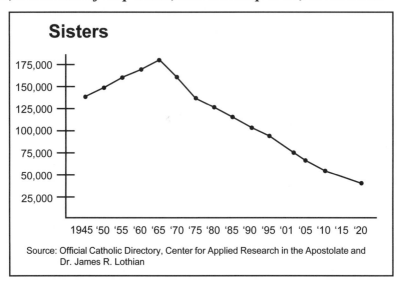

❖ *In 1965 there were 39.43 sisters for every 10,000 Catholics, in 2002 there were 11.56 — a decline of 71 percent.*

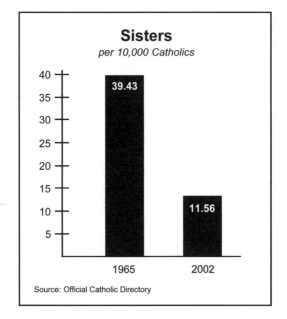

Sisters

Year	Sisters	Percentage Increase (Decrease)
1945	138,079	-
1950	147,310	07%
1955	158,069	07%
1960	168,527	07%
1965	179,954	07%
1970	160,931	(11%)
1975	135,225	(16%)
1980	126,517	(06%)
1985	115,386	(09%)
1990	103,269	(11%)
1995	92,107	(11%)
2002	75,500	(18%)
2005	65,318	(13%)
2010	53,518	(18%)
2020	39,282	(27%)

Source: Official Catholic Directory, Center for Applied Research in the Apostolate and Dr. James R. Lothian

❖ "The number of religious women in the database [in 1999] is 73,578. Of that number, 36,881 or 50% are age seventy or above, and 97.11% of those in that age group are receiving Social Security benefits. The number of religious men is 17,564 with 32% (5,673 priests and brothers) age seventy or above; 82.73% of those are receiving Social Security benefits." (*Retirement Fund for Religious Newsletter*, National Conference of Catholic Bishops, Spring 1999)

❖ "More than half of the women religious and about 35 percent of men religious in the country [in 2001] are now past age 70. ... The average age of women religious is 68 and the average age for men religious is 62." (*Annual Retirement Fund Helps Men, Women Religious*, St. Louis Review, Nov. 2, 2001)

❖ *By 2020, there will be only 21,792 sisters age 70 and under.*

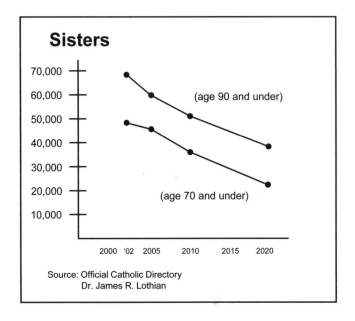

Year	Sisters Age 90 and under	Sisters Age 70 and under
2002	67,996	40,056
2005	60,602	36,063
2010	51,141	30,225
2020	37,791	21,792

Source: Official Catholic Directory
Dr. James R. Lothian

Chapter 2

Catholic Education

Catholic Schools

❖ *Between 1965 and 2002, the number of diocesan high schools decreased by 50 percent. There were more than twice as many diocesan high schools in 1945 as in 2002.*

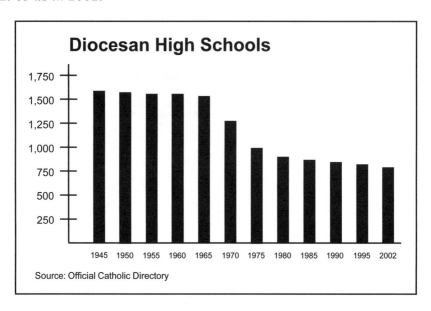

Diocesan High Schools

Year	High Schools	Percentage Increase (Decrease)
1920	-	-
1930	-	-
1940	-	-
1945	1,599	-
1950	1,576	(01%)
1955	1,557	(01%)
1960	1,567	01%
1965	1,566	00%
1970	1,265	(19%)
1975	995	(21%)
1980	894	(10%)
1985	870	(03%)
1990	839	(04%)
1995	823	(02%)
2002	786	(04%)

Source: Official Catholic Directory

❖ *Between 1965 and 2002, the number of private Catholic high schools decreased by 38 percent. There were more private Catholic high schools in 1945 than in 2002.*

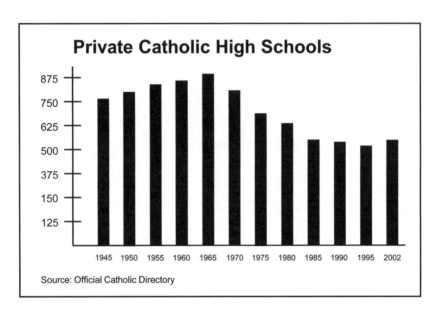

Private Catholic High Schools

Year	High Schools	Percentage Increase (Decrease)
1920	-	-
1930	-	-
1940	-	-
1945	762	-
1950	806	06%
1955	842	04%
1960	866	03%
1965	899	04%
1970	817	(09%)
1975	681	(17%)
1980	633	(07%)
1985	555	(12%)
1990	540	(03%)
1995	527	(02%)
2002	557	06%

Source: Official Catholic Directory

❖ *Between 1965 and 2002, the number of parochial grade schools decreased by 37 percent. There were more parochial grade schools in 1930 than in 2002.*

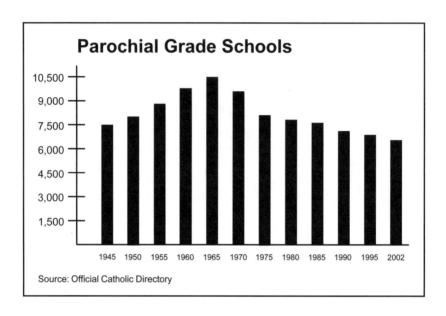

Parochial Grade Schools

Year	Grade Schools	Percentage Increase (Decrease)
1920	5,852	-
1930	7,225	23%
1940	7,597	05%
1945	7,493	(01%)
1950	7,914	06%
1955	8,843	12%
1960	9,897	12%
1965	10,503	06%
1970	9,601	(09%)
1975	8,199	(15%)
1980	7,847	(04%)
1985	7,658	(02%)
1990	7,273	(05%)
1995	6,911	(05%)
2002	6,623	(04%)

Source: Official Catholic Directory

❖ *Between 1965 and 2002, the number of private Catholic grade schools decreased by 24 percent. There were more private Catholic grade schools in 1945 than in 2002.*

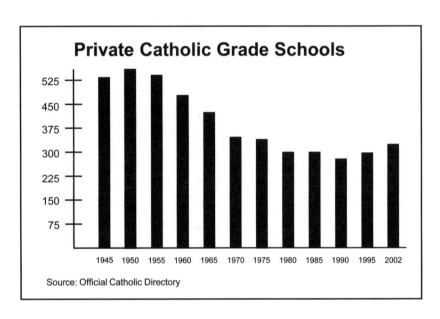

Private Catholic Grade Schools

Year	Grade Schools	Percentage Increase (Decrease)
1920	-	-
1930	-	-
1940	-	-
1945	537	-
1950	588	09%
1955	542	(08%)
1960	475	(12%)
1965	428	(10%)
1970	346	(19%)
1975	340	(02%)
1980	302	(11%)
1985	299	(01%)
1990	271	(09%)
1995	299	03%
2002	326	09%

Source: Official Catholic Directory

❖ *Between 1965 and 2002, the number of diocesan high school students decreased by 45 percent. There were more diocesan high school students in 1955 than in 2002.*

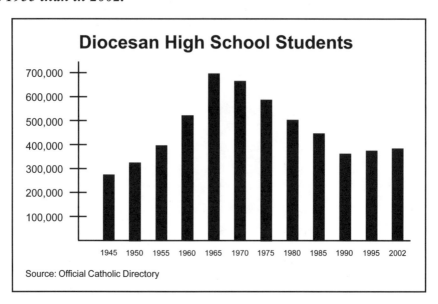

❖ *In 1965 there were 153 diocesan high school students for every 10,000 Catholics, in 2002 there were 61 — a decline of 60 percent.*

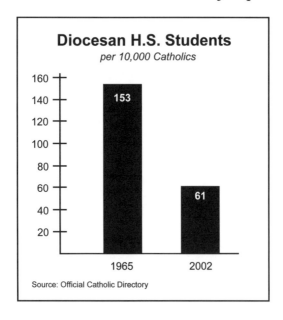

Diocesan High School Students

Year	Students	Percentage Increase (Decrease)
1920	-	-
1930	-	-
1940	-	-
1945	278,619	-
1950	324,398	16%
1955	398,192	23%
1960	520,128	31%
1965	698,032	34%
1970	667,408	(04%)
1975	590,495	(12%)
1980	505,955	(14%)
1985	478,044	(05%)
1990	365,834	(24%)
1995	378,847	04%
2002	386,157	02%

Source: Official Catholic Directory

❖ *Between 1965 and 2002, the number of private Catholic high school students decreased by 23 percent. There were more private Catholic high school students in 1960 than in 2002.*

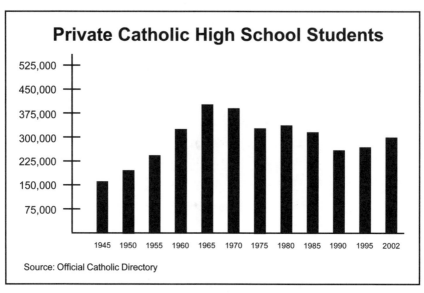

❖ *In 1965 there were 87 private high school students for every 10,000 Catholics, in 2002 there were 47 — a decline of 46 percent.*

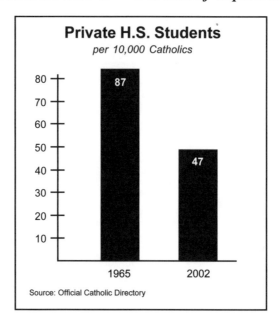

Private High School Students

Year	Students	Percentage Increase (Decrease)
1920	-	-
1930	-	-
1940	-	-
1945	169,080	-
1950	195,480	16%
1955	241,415	24%
1960	324,171	34%
1965	397,487	23%
1970	387,234	(03%)
1975	330,021	(15%)
1980	340,604	(03%)
1985	315,984	(07%)
1990	264,833	(16%)
1995	273,207	03%
2002	305,299	12%

Source: Official Catholic Directory

❖ *Between 1965 and 2002, the number of parochial grade school students decreased by 57 percent. There were more parochial grade school students in 1930 than in 2002.*

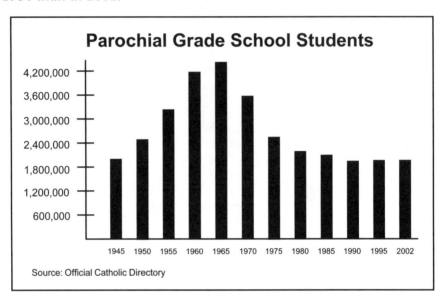

❖ *In 1965 there were 981 parochial grade school students for every 10,000 Catholics, in 2002 there were 294 — a decline of 70 percent.*

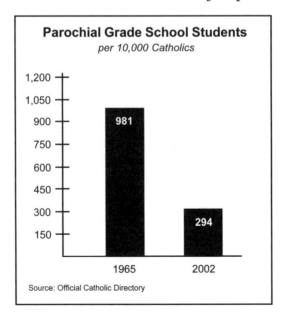

Parochial Grade School Students

Year	Students	Percentage Increase (Decrease)
1920	1,701,213	-
1930	2,248,571	21%
1940	2,108,892	(06%)
1945	2,029,012	(04%)
1950	2,477,741	22%
1955	3,253,608	31%
1960	4,195,781	30%
1965	4,476,881	07%
1970	3,598,096	(20%)
1975	2,535,406	(30%)
1980	2,251,294	(11%)
1985	2,100,578	(07%)
1990	1,920,340	(04%)
1995	1,949,989	02%
2002	1,918,853	(02%)

Source: Official Catholic Directory

❖ *Between 1965 and 2002, the number of private grade school students decreased by 4 percent.*

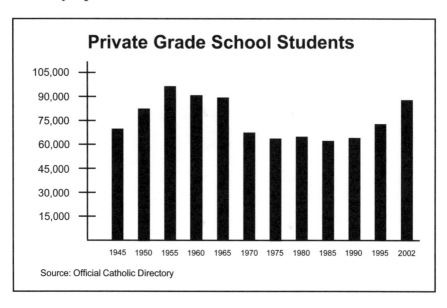

❖ *In 1965 there were 19.7 private grade school students for every 10,000 Catholics, in 2002 there were 13.3 — a decline of 32 percent.*

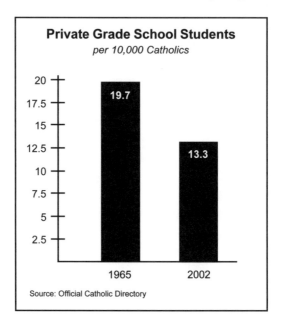

Private Grade School Students

Year	Students	Percentage Increase (Decrease)
1920	-	-
1930	-	-
1940	-	-
1945	69,986	-
1950	82,885	18%
1955	95,685	15%
1960	90,115	(06%)
1965	89,982	00%
1970	67,280	(25%)
1975	63,821	(05%)
1980	65,906	03%
1985	62,377	(05%)
1990	65,596	05%
1995	73,987	13%
2002	86,720	17%

Source: Official Catholic Directory

Teachers

❖ *Between 1965 and 2002, the number of sisters teaching decreased by 92 percent. There were over nine times as many sisters teaching in 1945 as in 2002.*

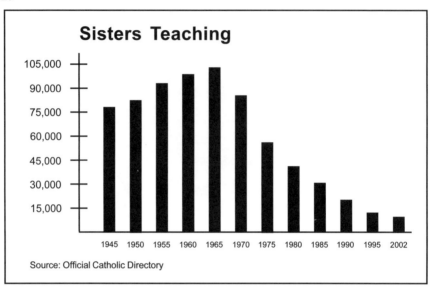

❖ *In 1965 there were 22.9 sisters teaching for every 10,000 Catholics, in 2002 there were 1.26 — a decline of 94 percent.*

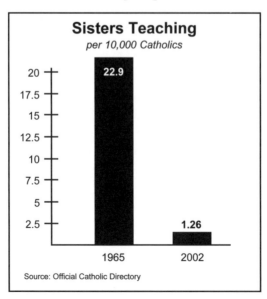

Sisters Teaching

Year	Sisters Teaching	Percentage Increase (Decrease)
1920	-	-
1930	-	-
1940	-	-
1945	77,874	-
1950	82,048	05%
1955	92,858	13%
1960	98,471	06%
1965	104,314	06%
1970	85,616	(18%)
1975	56,050	(35%)
1980	41,135	(27%)
1985	30,223	(27%)
1990	19,012	(37%)
1995	12,969	(32%)
2002	8,233	(37%)

Source: Official Catholic Directory

❖ In 1965, 58 percent of all sisters were teaching. By 2002 only 11 percent were teaching.

❖ *Between 1965 and 2002, the number of priests teaching decreased by 85 percent. There were over twice as many priests teaching in 1945 as in 2002.*

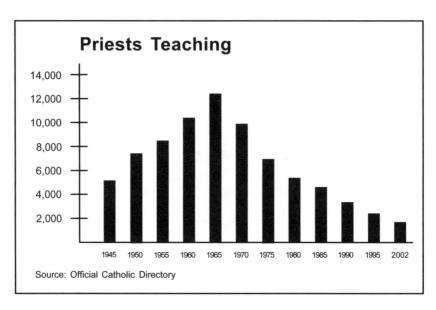

❖ *In 1965 there were 2.71 priests teaching for every 10,000 Catholics, in 2002 there was .30 — a decline of 89 percent.*

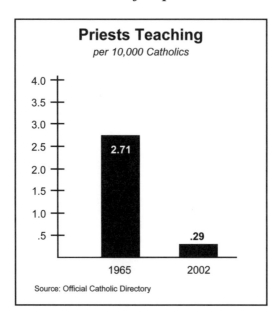

Catholic Education

Priests Teaching

Year	Priests Teaching	Percentage Increase (Decrease)
1920	-	-
1930	-	-
1940	-	-
1945	5,104	-
1950	7,436	46%
1955	8,513	14%
1960	10,890	28%
1965	12,346	13%
1970	9,958	(19%)
1975	6,974	(30%)
1980	5,444	(22%)
1985	4,600	(16%)
1990	3,317	(28%)
1995	2,440	(26%)
2002	1,899	(23%)

Source: Official Catholic Directory

❖ In 1965, 21 percent of all priests were teaching. By 2002 only 4 percent were teaching.

❖ *Between 1965 and 2002, the number of brothers teaching decreased by 80 percent. There were three times as many brothers teaching in 1945 as in 2002.*

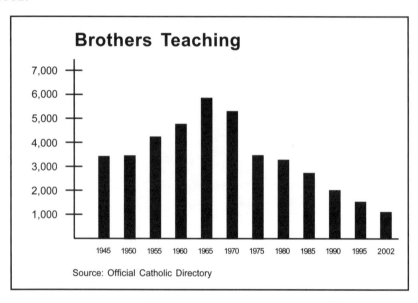

❖ *In 1965 there were 1.29 brothers teaching for every 10,000 Catholics, in 2002 there was .18 — a decline of 86 percent.*

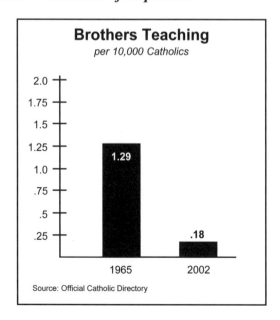

Brothers Teaching

Year	Brothers Teaching	Percentage Increase (Decrease)
1920	-	-
1930	-	-
1940	-	-
1945	3,371	-
1950	3,411	01%
1955	4,237	24%
1960	4,778	13%
1965	5,868	23%
1970	5,297	(10%)
1975	3,512	(34%)
1980	3,271	(07%)
1985	2,678	(18%)
1990	2,034	(24%)
1995	1,564	(23%)
2002	1,194	(24%)

Source: Official Catholic Directory

❖ In 1965, 48 percent of all brothers were teaching. By 2002 only 21 percent were teaching.

Chapter 3

Catholic Practice and Belief

❖ *Between 1965 and 2002, the number of infant baptisms decreased by 23 percent. There were more infant baptisms in 1955 than in 2002.*

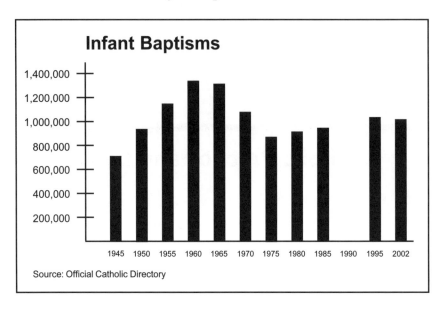

❖ *In 1965 there were 287 infant baptisms for every 10,000 Catholics, in 2002 there were 154 — a decline of 46 percent.*

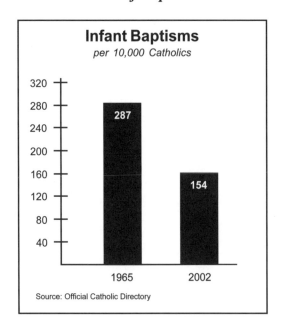

Infant Baptisms

Year	Baptisms	Percentage Increase (Decrease)
1920	-	-
1930	-	-
1940	-	-
1945	710,648	-
1950	943,443	33%
1955	1,161,304	23%
1960	1,344,576	16%
1965	1,310,413	(03%)
1970	1,086,858	(17%)
1975	876,306	(19%)
1980	910,506	04%
1985	947,668	04%
1990	-	-
1995	1,029,694	09%
2002	1,007,716	(02%)

Source: Official Catholic Directory

❖ *Between 1965 and 2002, the number of converts (adult baptisms) decreased by 37 percent. There were more converts in 1945 than in 2002.*

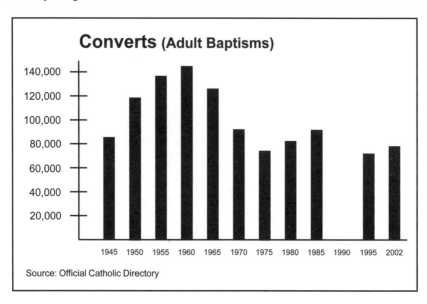

❖ *In 1965 there were 27.7 converts (adult baptisms) for every 10,000 Catholics, in 2002 there were 12.2 — a decline of 56 percent.*

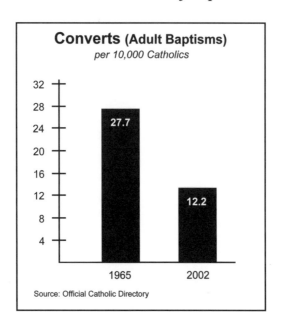

Catholic Practice and Belief

Converts (Adult Baptisms)

Year	Converts	Percentage Increase (Decrease)
1920	-	-
1930	38,232	-
1940	73,677	93%
1945	84,908	15%
1950	119,173	40%
1955	137,310	15%
1960	146,212	06%
1965	126,209	(05%)
1970	92,670	(27%)
1975	75,123	(19%)
1980	81,968	09%
1985	91,750	12%
1990	-	-
1995	73,332	(20%)
2002	79,892	09%

Source: Official Catholic Directory

❖ *Between 1965 and 2002, the number of Catholic marriages decreased by 27 percent. There were more marriages in 1950 than in 2002.*

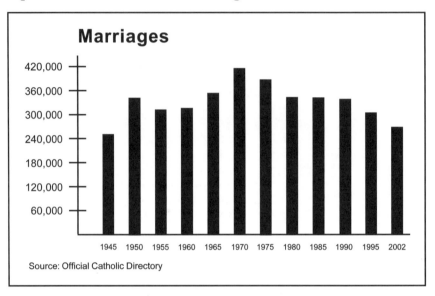

❖ *In 1965 there were 77.2 marriages for every 10,000 Catholics, in 2002 there were 39.3 — a decline of 49 percent.*

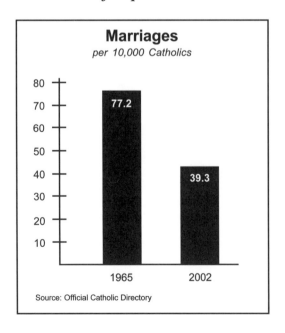

Marriages

Year	Marriages	Percentage Increase (Decrease)
1920	-	-
1930	-	-
1940	-	-
1945	249,140	-
1950	338,512	36%
1955	313,652	(07%)
1960	319,992	02%
1965	352,458	10%
1970	417,271	18%
1975	385,029	(08%)
1980	345,521	(10%)
1985	345,753	00%
1990	341,356	(01%)
1995	305,385	(11%)
2002	256,563	(16%)

Source: Official Catholic Directory

Annulments

❖ *There were virtually no annulments in the United States in 1968 (338). Thirty years later there were 50,498.*

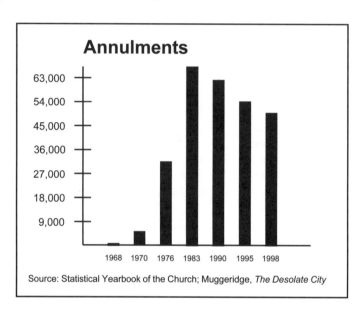

❖ "According to the 1994 *Catholic Almanac*, 59,220,000 American Catholics make up 6.2% of the world's 949,578,000 Catholic population. In 1991, the U.S. accounted for 63,900 (79%) of the world's 80,700 annulments." (*Annulments in America*, Edward Peters, *Homiletic and Pastoral Review*, November 1996)

Annulments

Year	Annulments	Percentage Increase (Decrease)
1968	338	-
1970	5,403	1322%
1976	30,324	461%
1983	66,417	119%
1990	62,924	(05%)
1995	54,013	(14%)
1998	50,498	(07%)

Source: Statistical Yearbook of the Church; Muggeridge, *The Desolate City*

Mass Attendance

❖ *According to Dr. James R. Lothian, about 65 percent of U.S. Catholics went to Sunday Mass in 1965, compared to 25 percent in 2000. Following are excerpts from Dr. Lothian's article in the October 2000 issue of the Homiletic and Pastoral Review, "Novus Ordo Missae: The Record After Thirty Years." Dr. Lothian is Distinguished Professor of Finance at Fordham University and editor of the Journal of International Money and Finance.*

I have collected data on Mass attendance of U.S. Catholics over the period 1939 to 1995. I compare these data with data on Mass attendance of English and Welsh Catholics over the shorter period 1959 to 1996 and with data on church attendance of U.S. Protestants over the same period as for U.S. Catholics.

The picture that emerges is distressing. Mass attendance of U.S. Catholics fell precipitously in the decade following the liturgical changes and has continued to decline ever since. This decline moreover is not an isolated phenomenon, confined solely to the Church in America. In England and Wales, the time pattern of Mass attendance has been just as bad, perhaps even worse. Church attendance of Protestants, in contrast, has followed a much different path. For most of the period it was without any discernible trend, either up or down. In recent years it actually has risen. The notion that the Catholic fall off was simply one part of a larger societal trend, therefore, receives absolutely no support in these data.

Shown in Figure 1 are the data for the U.S. Catholics for the period 1939 to 1995 and for English and Welsh Catholics for the period 1959 to 1996. The U.S. data are survey data compiled by Gallup (1995, 1996). The English and Welsh data are from parish records as reported in Currie, et al. (1977) and Joyce (1999)....

After temporarily rising to nearly 75% in the immediate aftermath of World War II, U.S. Mass attendance stood at about 65%, and hence roughly its 1939 level, in the period immediately surrounding Vatican II. From there on, it fell continuously, at a relatively fast pace initially, then much more slowly, and now more recently faster again. In 1995, according to these data, it stood at 46%, which as we will see below is about the same level as Protestant Church attendance in the United Sates in that year. ...

The data on Mass attendance in England and Wales, which also are plotted in Figure 1, are used to address the question of data representativeness. With two small exceptions, this series follows a similar path to that of the U.S. series. Again there is a substantial initial decline – roughly 15 percentage points – in the

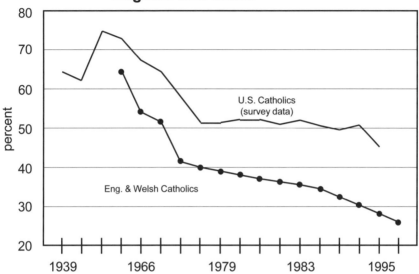

Figure 1. Mass attendance in the U.S. and in England and Wales

decade or so surrounding Vatican II, followed by a slower paced, but nevertheless continual decline thereafter. Over the period as a whole, Mass attendance in England and Wales fell by almost 29 percentage points, about the same as in the United States. The differences between the two series are the consistently lower reported level of Mass attendance in England and Wales than in the United States, and the somewhat more rapid rate of decline in England and Wales than in the United States in the latter half of the period.

Fitting a trend line to the English and Welsh data, I obtained an estimate of the annual rate of change of minus .8 percentage points per year. As in the case of the U.S., the probability of obtaining this estimate when the true trend rate of change was zero turned out to be exceedingly low – less than two tenths of one per cent.

Now let me turn to the issue of measurement error. As already mentioned, the U.S. data are survey data. Their accuracy, therefore, in part depends upon the truthfulness of survey responses. A problem of some potential importance here is bias in the U.S. survey caused by some Catholics who did not attend Mass in the weeks in question claiming that they did. Using headcount data like those for England and Wales is one way to solve this problem, but such are data not available for the United States in a continuous form. Two independent scholars,

Professors Mark Chaves and James Cavendish (1994), however, have compiled such data for the year 1994 alone. The estimate that they come up with for that year is 25 per cent attendance versus the 46 per cent figure given in the 1995 Gallup survey.

One obviously cannot just lump this figure together with the earlier Gallup data since the latter almost certainly contain a systematic bias also. It is, however, possible to use the Chaves and Cavendish estimate together with the Gallup figure for 1994 to adjust the earlier Gallup data for this apparent bias. I did this by assuming that the ratio of those who did not attend Mass according to Chaves and Cavendish but claimed that they did to the total number of non-attendees was the same in the earlier years as in the mid-1990s. I estimated this ratio using the Chaves and Cavendish figure for 1994 in combination with the Gallup figure for 1995. I then applied this estimate to the earlier Gallup data to arrive at the adjusted series plotted in Figure 2.

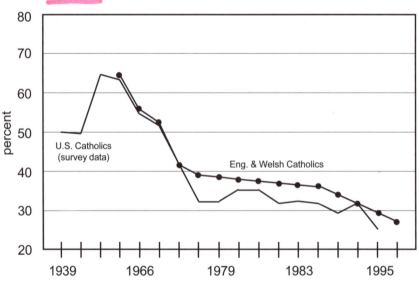

Figure 2. Mass attendance, adjusted U.S. data

Three features of this new series stand out. The first is its much lower level throughout the period. The second is the near coincidence between this series and the series for England and Wales. The third is the greater total decline in U.S. Mass attendance implied by this series as opposed to the survey-based series.

The data, therefore, confirm what casual impressions for some time have suggested. Mass attendance is way down, even in America and Britain where the Church had been strong. To make matters worse it continues to fall further....

Correlation versus causation

Such a conclusion, it could be argued, confuses correlation and temporal ordering with causation. The observed trends may very well be real but have little to do with the post-conciliar liturgical changes *per se*. They could instead be a reflection of other factors. The declines in Mass attendance could conceivably be just one further consequence of the broader erosion of values that began in the late 1960s, and that has continued thereafter.

The data on church attendance of U.S. Protestants, which are plotted in Figure 3 together with the data for Catholics that we have just reviewed, provide evidence on this question. The Protestant series is, so to speak, the 'control group.' The contrast between its behavior and those of the two Catholic series is stark indeed. In the Protestant data, we see no downward trend at all. Church attendance is lower than that for Catholics during most of the period but is certainly not declining. In fact it may even have begun to trend up. If the temper of the times had been the cause of the decline in Catholic Mass attendance however, there is no reason that similar forces should not have operated within Protestantism too. Church attendance should have declined there also.

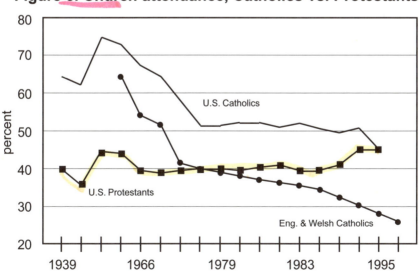

Figure 3. Church attendance, Catholics vs. Protestants

Statistical tests applied to the three series reinforce these conclusions. They showed a less than one in ten-thousandth of a percent chance of the estimated trend rates of change for the two Catholic series and for the Protestant series being equal. The bottom line then is that the downward trends in the two Catholic series and the lack of a similar trend in the Protestant series appear to be behavioral phenomena, and not fluke occurrences.

This is a powerful finding, and quite at odds with the conventional view. If the post-conciliar changes had been the overwhelming success they very often are described as being, we would expect to see increases in Mass attendance. We would certainly not expect to see the substantial declines that have taken place in both the United States and England and Wales over the past 30 years. That Protestant church attendance during this period behaved so differently makes the data even more difficult to reconcile with the conventional view. Had Protestant church attendance declined too, it might have been possible to argue that the situation in Catholicism would have been even worse if the liturgical changes had not been implemented. Given the near constancy and then rise in Protestant attendance, however, that argument becomes quite tenuous, if not out and out untenable.

❖ *According to other studies of Mass attendance, the percentage of Catholics who attend weekly Mass varies according to the poll and the year.*

1958 Gallup Poll: 74 percent
1988 Gallup Poll: 48 percent
1994 Notre Dame study: 26.6 percent[x]
1999 National Catholic Reporter: 37 percent (total Catholics); 27 percent (ages 18-38); 42 percent (ages 39-58); 64 percent (ages 59 plus)
2000 Roper Poll: 57 percent
2001 Zogby Poll: 54 percent

❖ *Only 10 percent of Catholics go to confession at least once a month, 33 percent go less than once a year, and 10 percent say they have never been to confession.* (Catholic World Report/Roper Poll, 1997)

Polls of Catholics

Being a Good Catholic

Percentage of Catholics who believe a person can be a good Catholic without performing the following actions.

	1987	1993	1999
Without going to Church every Sunday	70	73	77
Without obeying Church teaching on birth control	66	73	72
Without obeying Church teaching on divorce and remarriage	57	62	65
Without obeying Church teaching on abortion	39	56	53
Without believing that in the Mass, the bread and wine actually become the Body and Blood of Jesus	--	--	38
Without their marriage being approved by the Catholic Church	51	61	68
Without donating their time or money to help the poor	44	52	56
Without donating their time or money to help the parish	--	57	60
Without believing that Jesus physically rose from the dead	--	--	23

Source: National Catholic Reporter, Oct. 29, 1999

Beliefs of Young Catholics

Percentage of Catholics ages 20 to 39 who believe that the following elements are "essential to the faith."

Belief that only men can be priests	17
Teachings that oppose abortion	31
Private confession to a priest	32
Obligation to attend Mass weekly	37
Devotion to the Saints	41
Regular daily prayer life	41
Christ establishes bishops through Peter	42
Necessity of having a pope	48
Having religious orders	48
Belief that Christ is Really Present in the Eucharist	58
Belief that God is present in the Sacraments	65

Source: Center for Applied Research in the Apostolate Report, Fall 2001

Beliefs of Catholic Elementary School Religion Teachers

Percentage of lay religion teachers in Catholic elementary schools who identify the Church's position on the following issues with their own.

Issue	%
Artificial birth control	10
Human and divine authorship of the Bible	19
Elective abortion	26
Infallibility of the Pope	27
Church moral teaching	28
Euthanasia	31
Male priesthood	33
Establishment of the hierarchy of the Church	41
Indissolubility of marriage	54
Real presence of the Eucharist	63
Afterlife	74
Existence of the devil	74
Resurrection	87
Divinity of Jesus	91
God's existence	98

Source: The Catholic Character of Catholic Schools, University of Notre Dame Press, 2000

❖ "In a [September 1995] poll conducted by *Time* and CNN, 76 percent of Catholics disagree that using artificial means of birth control is wrong. Seventy-nine percent say it is possible for Catholics to make up their own minds on these issues, and 80 percent believe it is possible to disagree with the pope on official positions on morality and still be a good Catholic. Only 15 percent of Catholics say a Catholic should always obey official church teachings on such moral issues as contraception and abortion. A *US News & World Report* survey reports similar findings — 82 percent of Catholics disapprove or strongly disapprove of the statement that using artificial birth control, such as condoms or birth control pills, is morally wrong." (*Humanae Vitae: Thirty Years of Discord and Dissent*, Megan Hartman, *Conscience*, Autumn 1999)

❖ Percentage of Catholics who believe the Eucharist is merely a "symbolic reminder" of Jesus:
Catholics age 65 and older: 45 percent
Catholics age 45-65: 58 percent
Catholics age 18-44: 70 percent
Catholics who attend Mass every Sunday: 51 percent
(New York Times/CBS Poll, 1994)

❖ "Despite clear and repeated statement from the magisterium indicating that women cannot be ordained to the priesthood, a majority of Catholics dissent on that issue ... with 42 percent saying that they 'strongly disagree' with the Chuch teaching, and another 16 percent that they 'mildly disagree.' Only 20 percent strongly agreed." (Catholic World Report/Roper Poll, 1997)

❖ "A [1992] New York Times poll shows that eight out of ten Catholics in the United States disagree with the statement, 'Using artificial means of birth control is wrong.' According to a Gallup poll, 87 percent of Catholic laity in the United States feel the church should permit couples to make their own decisions regarding birth control. (*Humanae Vitae: Thirty Years of Discord and Dissent*, Megan Hartman, *Conscience*, Autumn 1999)

❖ According to a Gallup poll, "Sixty-seven percent agree that 'it would be a good thing if women were allowed to be ordained as priests,' up from 47 percent in 1985 and 29 percent in 1974. An even higher percentage (75 percent) support a married priesthood. ... Eighty-seven percent say couples should make their own decision on birth control and 75 percent think divorced and remarried Catholics without annulments should be able to receive Communion." (*Bishops Meet at Notre Dame*, Thomas J. Reese, *America*, July 1, 1992)

❖ "When asked whether 'it is morally wrong to use artificial methods of birth control,' 57 percent strongly disagreed, and another 16 percent mildly disagreed, yielding an overall 73 percent objection to Catholic teaching." (Catholic World Report/Roper Poll, 1997)

❖ "In a [1994] poll conducted by the New York Times, 68 percent of US Catholic laity say they believe that someone who practices some form of birth control can still be a good Catholic. A Los Angeles Times poll reveals that opposition to contraception among clergy and women religious is also much lower than the hierarchy would like. Only 49 percent of priests and and 37 percent of women religious said it is always or often a sin for a married couple to use a form of artificial contraception. (*Humanae Vitae: Thirty Years of Discord and Dissent*, Megan Hartman, *Conscience*, Autumn 1999)

❖ "[A]mong those who attend Mass at least once a week, ... even when those who 'mildly' agree are included in the calculations, only 46 percent accept Church teaching on abortion; 43 percent accept the all-male priesthood; and a paltry 30 percent recognize contraception as morally wrong." (Catholic World Report/Roper Poll, 1997)

❖ "A 1992 Gallup poll showed that 80 percent of U.S. Catholics disagreed with the statement 'Using artificial means of birth control is wrong.' And a 1996 study conducted by Father Thomas Sweetser for the Parish Evaluation Project found only 9 percent of Catholics ... consider birth control to be wrong." (U.S. Catholic, June 1998)

❖ "In a [1998] survey conducted by US Catholic, 81 percent of Catholics believe a married couple has the right to follow their own conscience on the decision to use birth control. Forty percent say Humanae Vitae was a mistake." (*Humanae Vitae: Thirty Years of Discord and Dissent*, Megan Hartman, *Conscience*, Autumn 1999)

❖ "The results [of a 2001 Roper Poll] show that 39 percent of the Catholic Americans 'strongly disagree' with the statement that 'abortion is never justified,' while another 20% 'mildly disagree.' Only 26 percent strongly embraced the Church's unequivocal pro-life position." (Catholic World Report/Roper Poll, 1997)

Chapter 4

Religious Orders

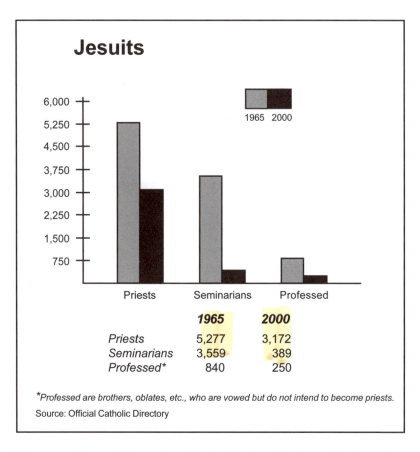

The number of Jesuit priests in the United States decreased by 40 percent between 1965 and 2000. The number of seminarians decreased by 89 percent.

❖ "As of January 2000, there were 21,354 Jesuits in the world – 15,020 priests (208 fewer than in 1999), 3,997 scholastics (35 fewer) and 2,311 brothers (75 fewer). The net loss from January 1999 is 320 members. Between January 1999 and January 2000, 522 men entered the Society of Jesus, 496 died and 341 left the order. The highest number of Jesuits in their 460 year history was in 1965 with 36,038 members – 20,301 priests, 9,865 scholastics and 5,872 brothers." (Jesuit Documentation No. 80)

Religious Orders

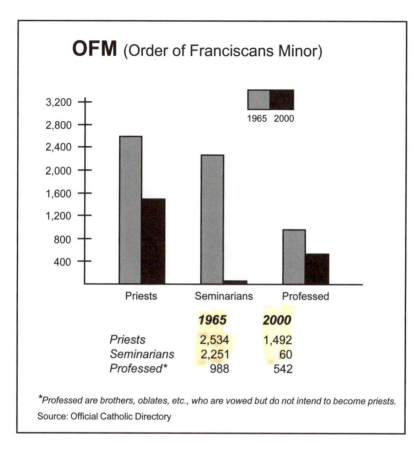

	1965	2000
Priests	2,534	1,492
Seminarians	2,251	60
Professed*	988	542

*Professed are brothers, oblates, etc., who are vowed but do not intend to become priests.
Source: Official Catholic Directory

The number of OFM priests in the United States decreased by 41 percent between 1965 and 2000. The number of seminarians decreased by 97 percent.

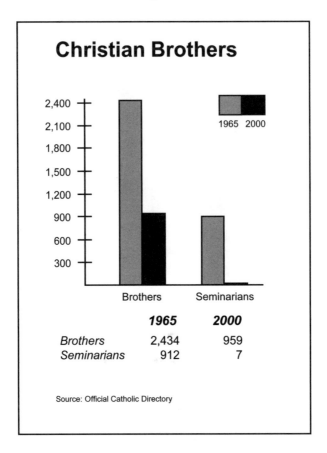

The number of Christian Brothers in the United States decreased by 61 percent between 1965 and 2000. The number of seminarians decreased by 99 percent.

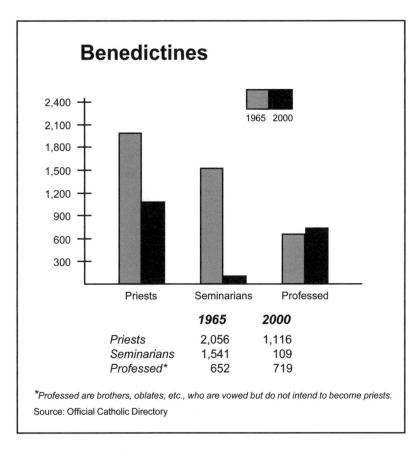

The number of Benedictine priests in the United States decreased by 40 percent between 1965 and 2000. The number of seminarians decreased by 93 percent.

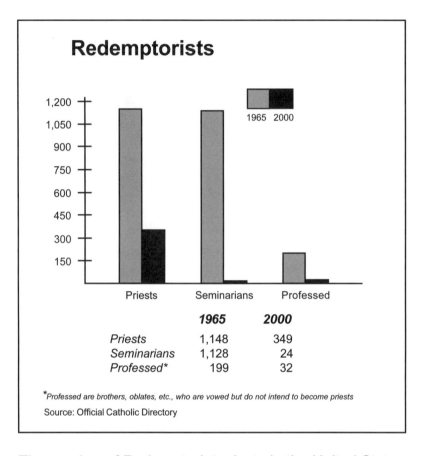

The number of Redemptorist priests in the United States decreased by 70 percent between 1965 and 2000. The number of seminarians decreased by 98 percent.

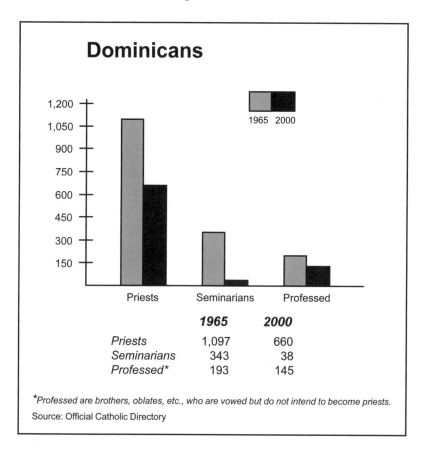

The number of Dominican priests in the United States decreased by 40 percent between 1965 and 2000. The number of seminarians decreased by 89 percent.

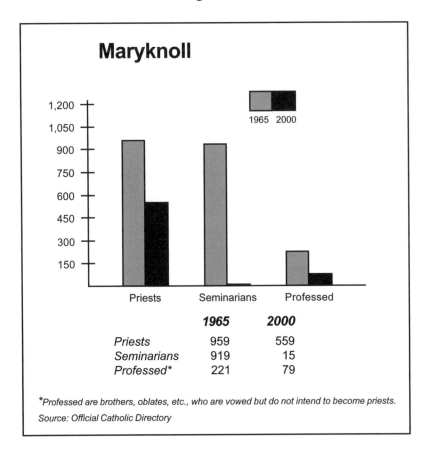

The number of Maryknoll priests in the United States decreased by 42 percent between 1965 and 2000. The number of seminarians decreased by 98 percent.

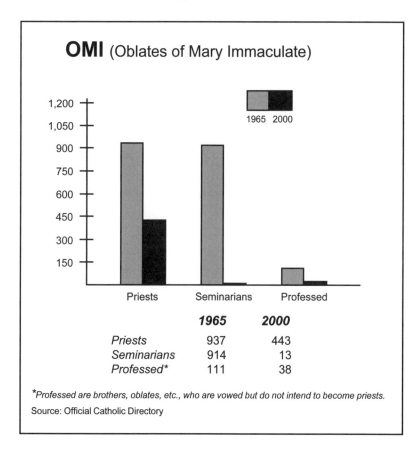

The number of OMI priests in the United States decreased by 53 percent between 1965 and 2000. The number of seminarians decreased by 99 percent.

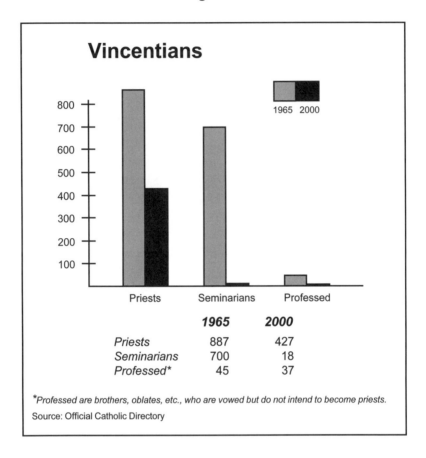

The number of Vincentian priests in the United States decreased by 52 percent between 1965 and 2000. The number of seminarians decreased by 97 percent.

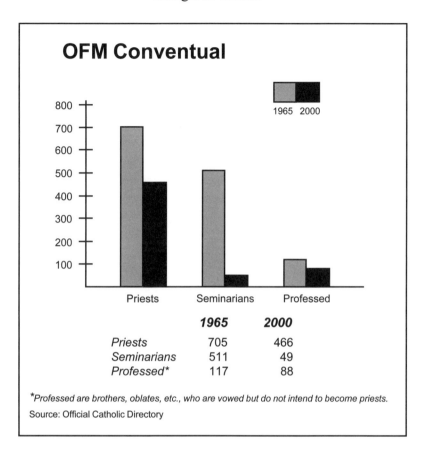

*Professed are brothers, oblates, etc., who are vowed but do not intend to become priests.
Source: Official Catholic Directory

The number of OFM Conventual priests in the United States decreased by 34 percent between 1965 and 2000. The number of seminarians decreased by 90 percent.

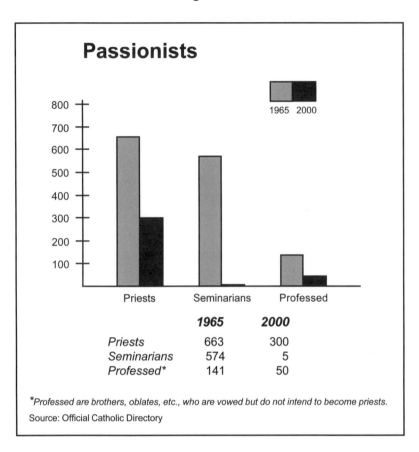

The number of Passionist priests in the United States decreased by 55 percent between 1965 and 2000. The number of seminarians decreased by 99 percent.

Religious Orders

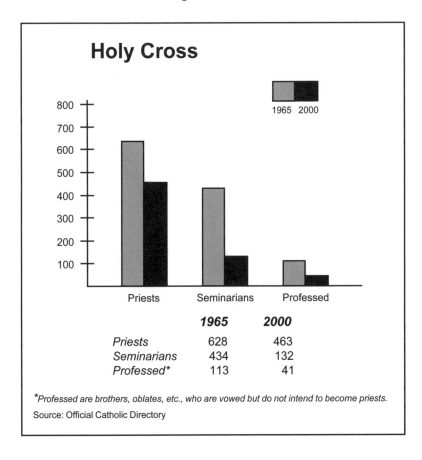

Holy Cross

	1965	*2000*
Priests	628	463
Seminarians	434	132
*Professed**	113	41

*Professed are brothers, oblates, etc., who are vowed but do not intend to become priests.
Source: Official Catholic Directory

The number of Holy Cross priests in the United States decreased by 26 percent between 1965 and 2000. The number of seminarians decreased by 70 percent.

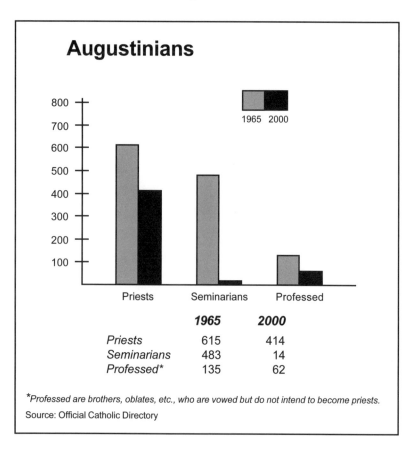

The number of Augustinian priests in the United States decreased by 33 percent between 1965 and 2000. The number of seminarians decreased by 97 percent.

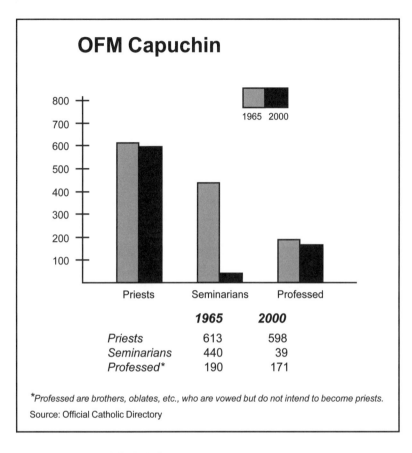

The number of OFM Capuchin priests in the United States decreased by 2 percent between 1965 and 2000. The number of seminarians decreased by 91 percent.

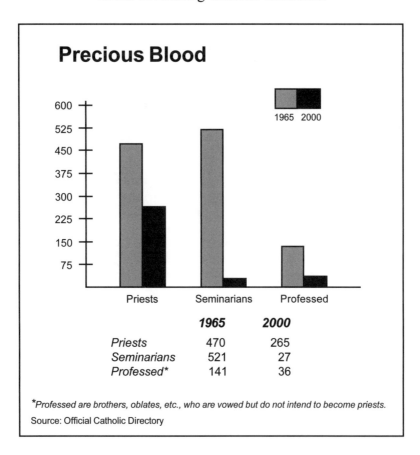

The number of Precious Blood priests in the United States decreased by 44 percent between 1965 and 2000. The number of seminarians decreased by 95 percent.

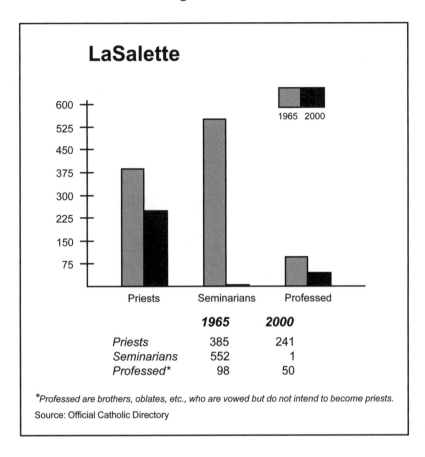

The number of LaSalette priests in the United States decreased by 37 percent between 1965 and 2000. The number of seminarians decreased by 99 percent.

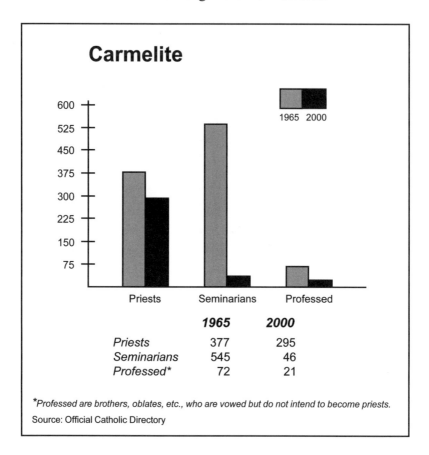

The number of Carmelite priests in the United States decreased by 21 percent between 1965 and 2000. The number of seminarians decreased by 92 percent.

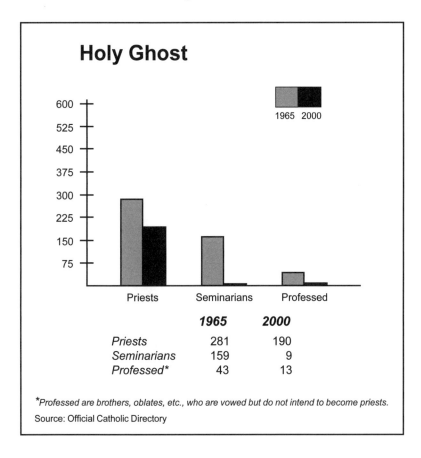

The number of Holy Ghost priests in the United States decreased by 32 percent between 1965 and 2000. The number of seminarians decreased by 94 percent.

Chapter 5

Canada and Europe

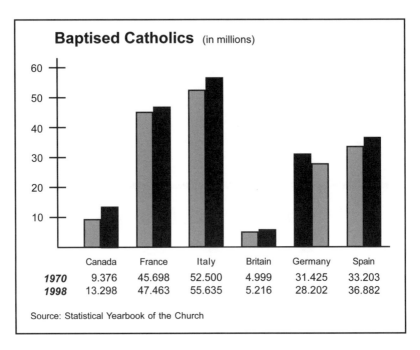

❖ "The dechristianization of Europe is a reality." – Cardinal Paul Poupard, President of the Pontifical Council for Culture (*Le Spectacle du Monde*, January 2000)

❖ "It's chic to declare yourself a Protestant in France these days. In intellectual circles, it is also chic to reveal yourself as a Jew. But if you admit to being a Roman Catholic, you'll trigger howls of derisive laughter." –Sociologist Daniele Hervieu-Leger (UPI, March 13, 2001)

❖ "Christianity as a background to people's lives and moral decisions and to the Government and to the social life of Britain has almost been vanquished. We live in a totally new time for all Christians, especially for we Catholics, and the anguish of the Western world is there for all to see." –Cardinal Cormac Murphy-O'Connor, Archbishop of Westminster (Sept. 5, 2001)

❖ "The number of [Irish] diocesan clergy has steadily declined over the past 20 years. From a high of 3,998 in 1980, it fell to 3,616 last year. The number of priests in religious orders has shown an even sharper drop, from 8,020 in 1965 to 6,912 in 1980 and 4,089 in 1996.

"In 1965, 282 young men were ordained as diocesan priests, while 377 were ordained into religious orders. Last year, those figures had fallen to 53 and 32 respectively. Two years ago, there were just 7,727 secular and religious clergy in

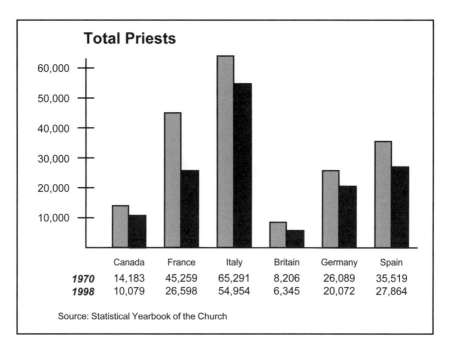

Ireland, serving a Catholic population of almost four million. ... Last year Dublin lost 19 priests and ordained two. ...

"Last year, for the first time ever, Holy Cross – the diocesan seminary for Dublin, which serves half the country's Catholics – did not receive a single entrant. There are now only 11 seminarians in the college. ... The national [Irish] seminary at Maynooth had just 21 entrants last year – the lowest figure in its history. Even the Pontifical Irish College in Rome is feeling the pinch. The College, which was founded in 1578, has 28 seminarians: 19 Irish and nine of other nationalities. The college is now taking students from Korea and eastern European countries like Slovakia and Rumania, where vocations have soared.'" (*Going the Distance*, Patrick Madrid, *Envoy Magazine*, July/August 1998)

❖ "Without priests the sacramental nature of the Church will disappear. We'll become a Protestant church without the sacraments." – Cardinal Godfried Daneels (London Catholic Times, May 2000)

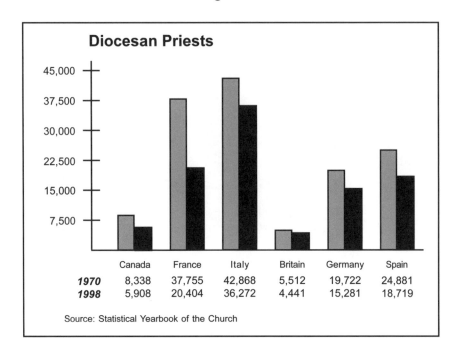

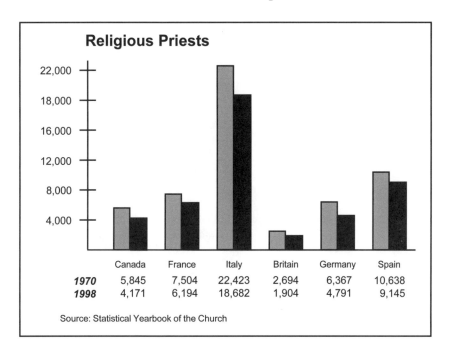

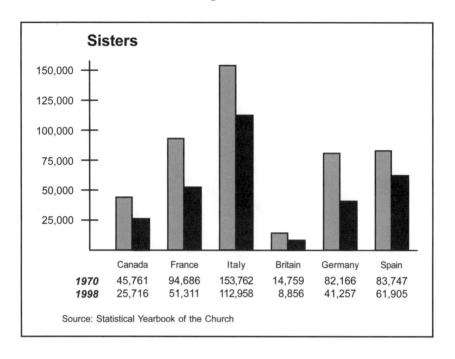

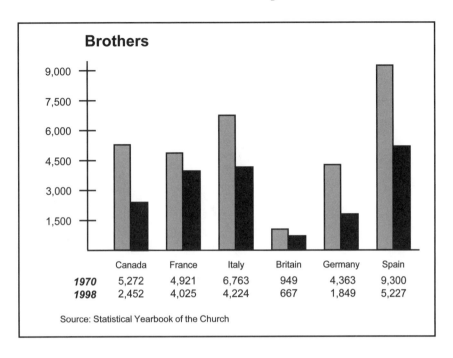

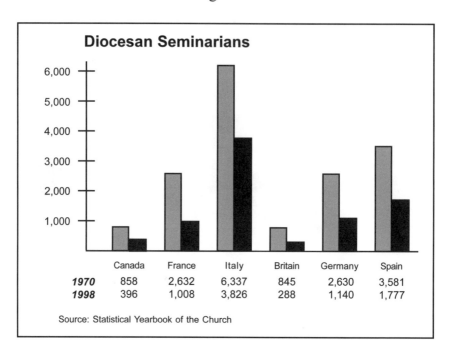

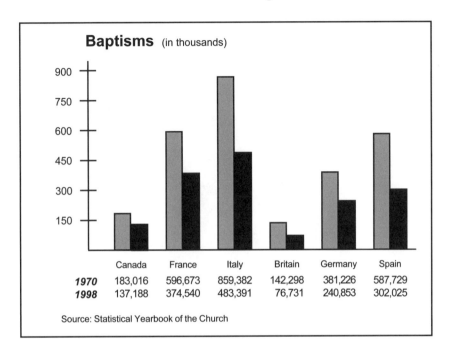

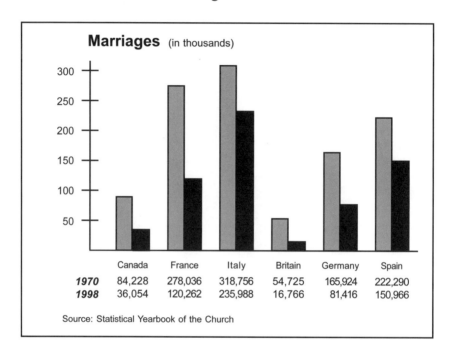

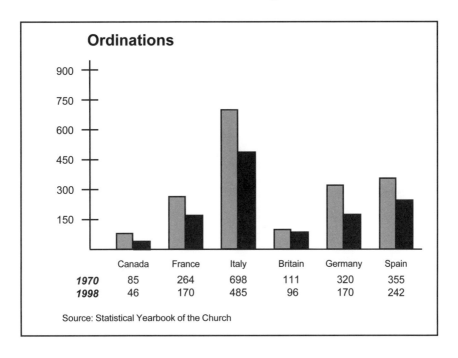

Kenneth C. Jones, an attorney, lives in St. Louis with his wife and seven children. He holds a bachelor's degree in government from the University of Notre Dame and earned his law degree from Washington University in St. Louis.